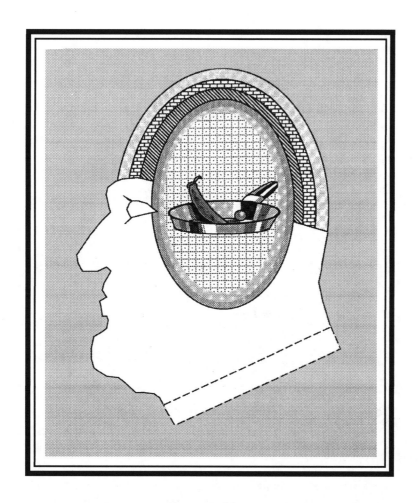

Cross Section of the Corporate Cranium

...as well as other
brainy cartoonish revelations
by Roy Schlemme

authorHOUSE

AuthorHouse™
1663 Liberty Drive
Bloomington, IN 47403
www.authorhouse.com
Phone: 833-262-8899

Published by AuthorHouse 04/16/2021

ISBN: 978-1-6655-1455-2 (sc)
ISBN: 978-1-6655-1458-3 (e)

Library of Congress Control Number: 2021901358

Print information available on the last page.

For Nancy & Lowell.

A little light visual amusement awaits...

...over the next 126 pages
(provided you don't nod off or
get distracted by the real world
somewhere along the way).
Would an award-winning designer
with an extended history of
creating out-of-the-ordinary
graphic entertainment lie to you?
Judge for yourself and,
hopefully, 'Enjoy'!

—*Roy Schlemme*

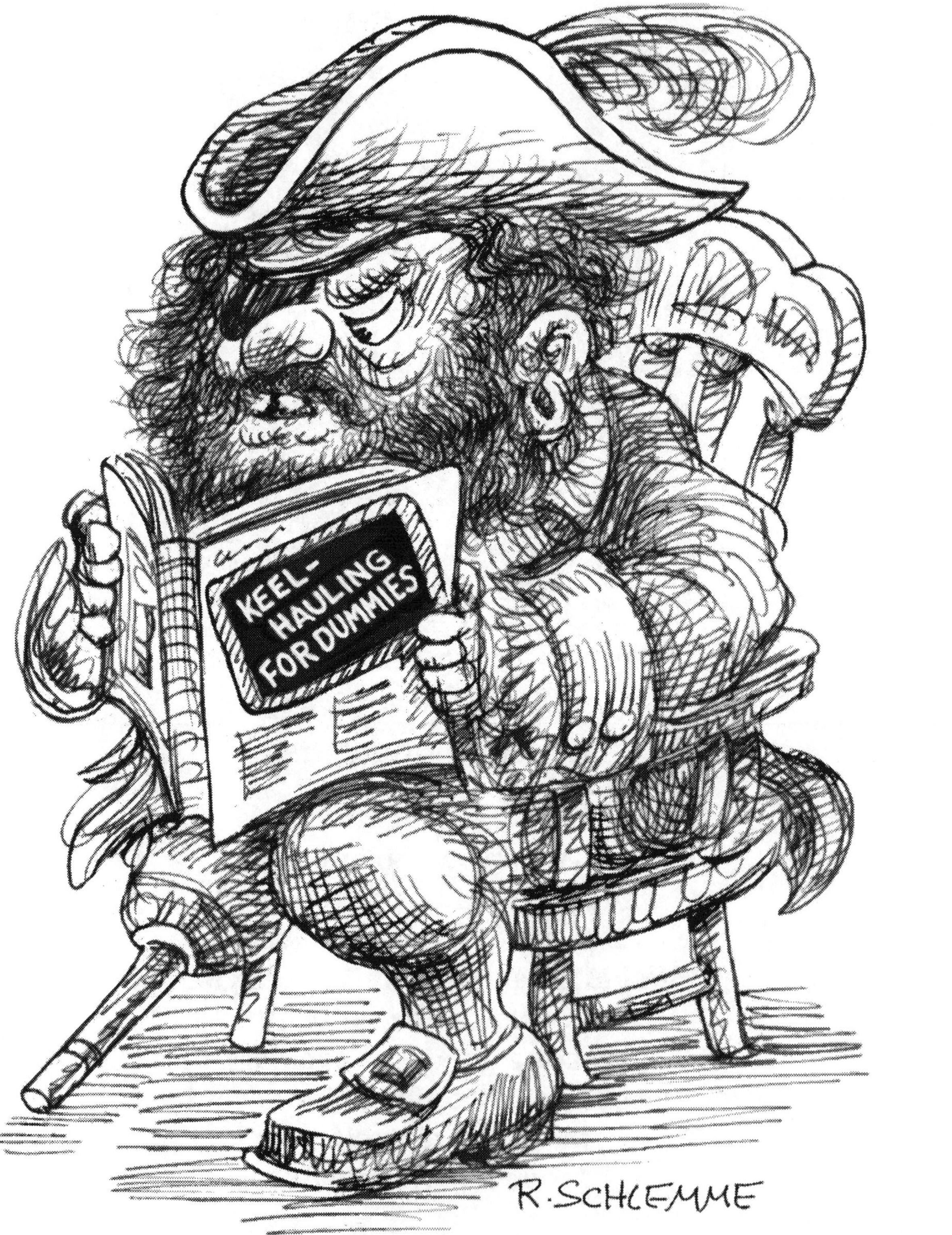
KEEL-
HAULING
FOR DUMMIES
R.SCHLEMME

"It's nearly unanimous, your majesty."

WHERE "THE BUDS" HANG OUT.

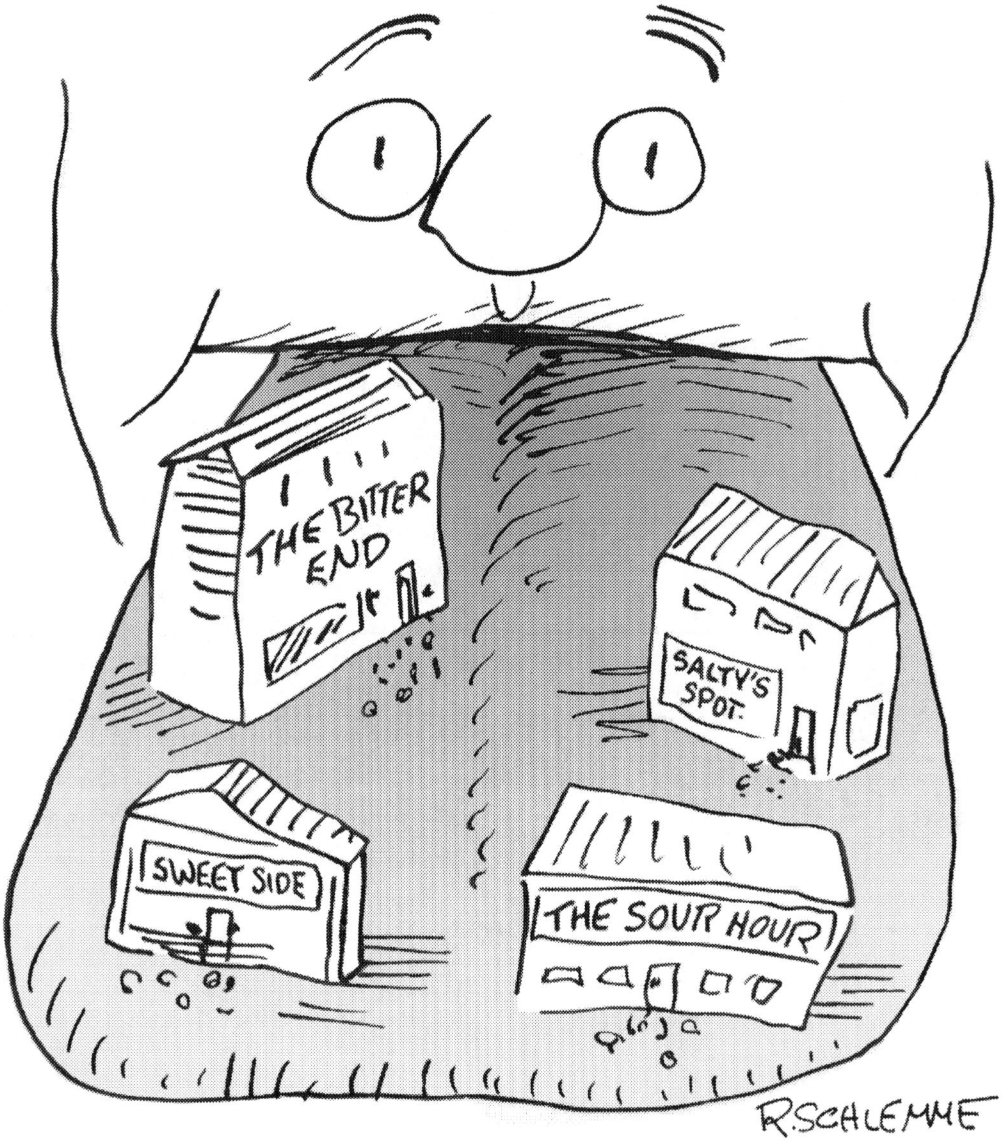
THE BITTER END
SALTY'S SPOT.
SWEET SIDE
THE SOUR HOUR
R.SCHLEMME

"Well, I clearly remember your telling me
you'd enjoy a little chicken for dinner."

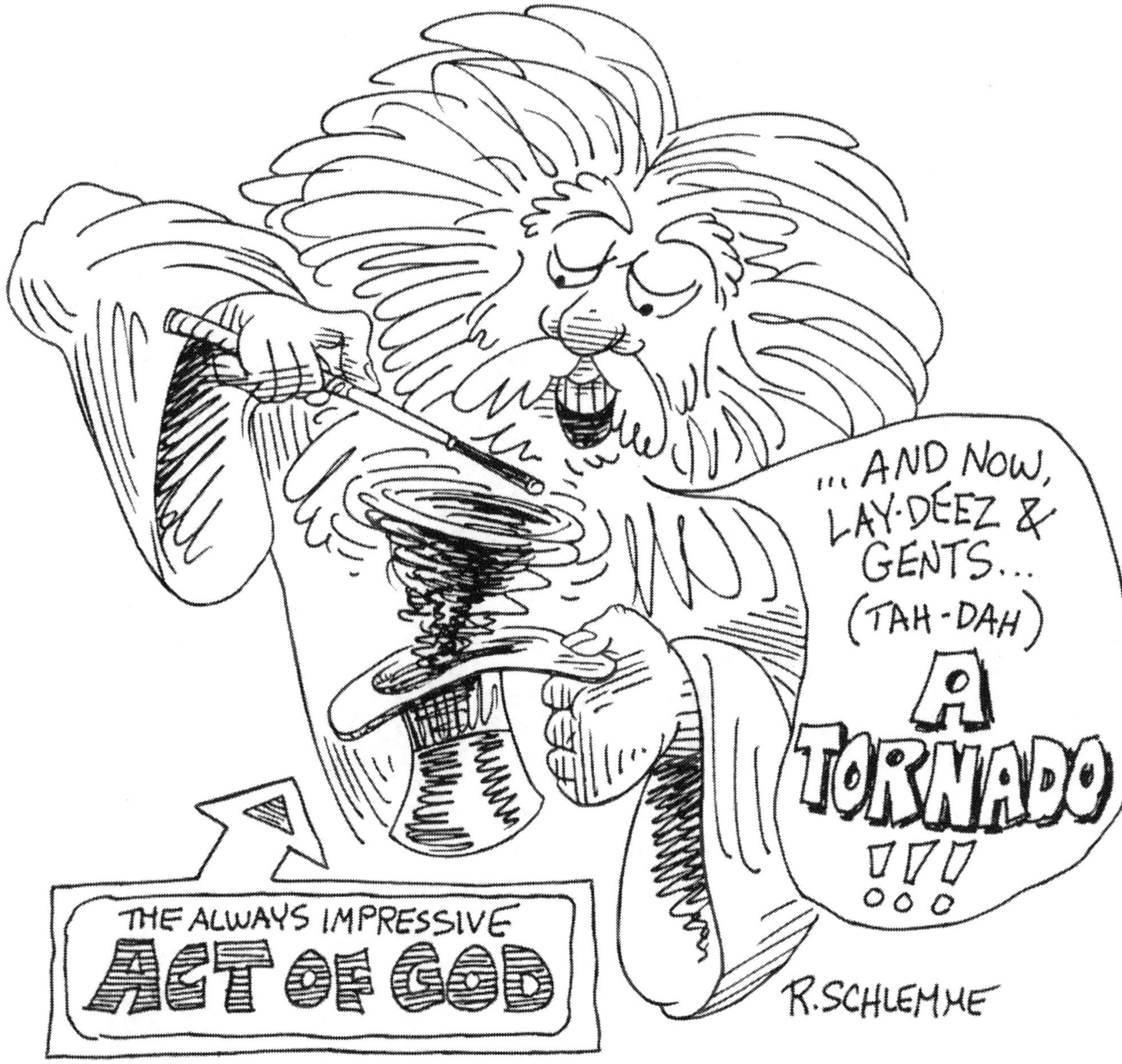
... AND NOW, LAY-DEEZ & GENTS... (TAH-DAH)
A TORNADO !!!
THE ALWAYS IMPRESSIVE
ACT OF GOD
R. SCHLEMME

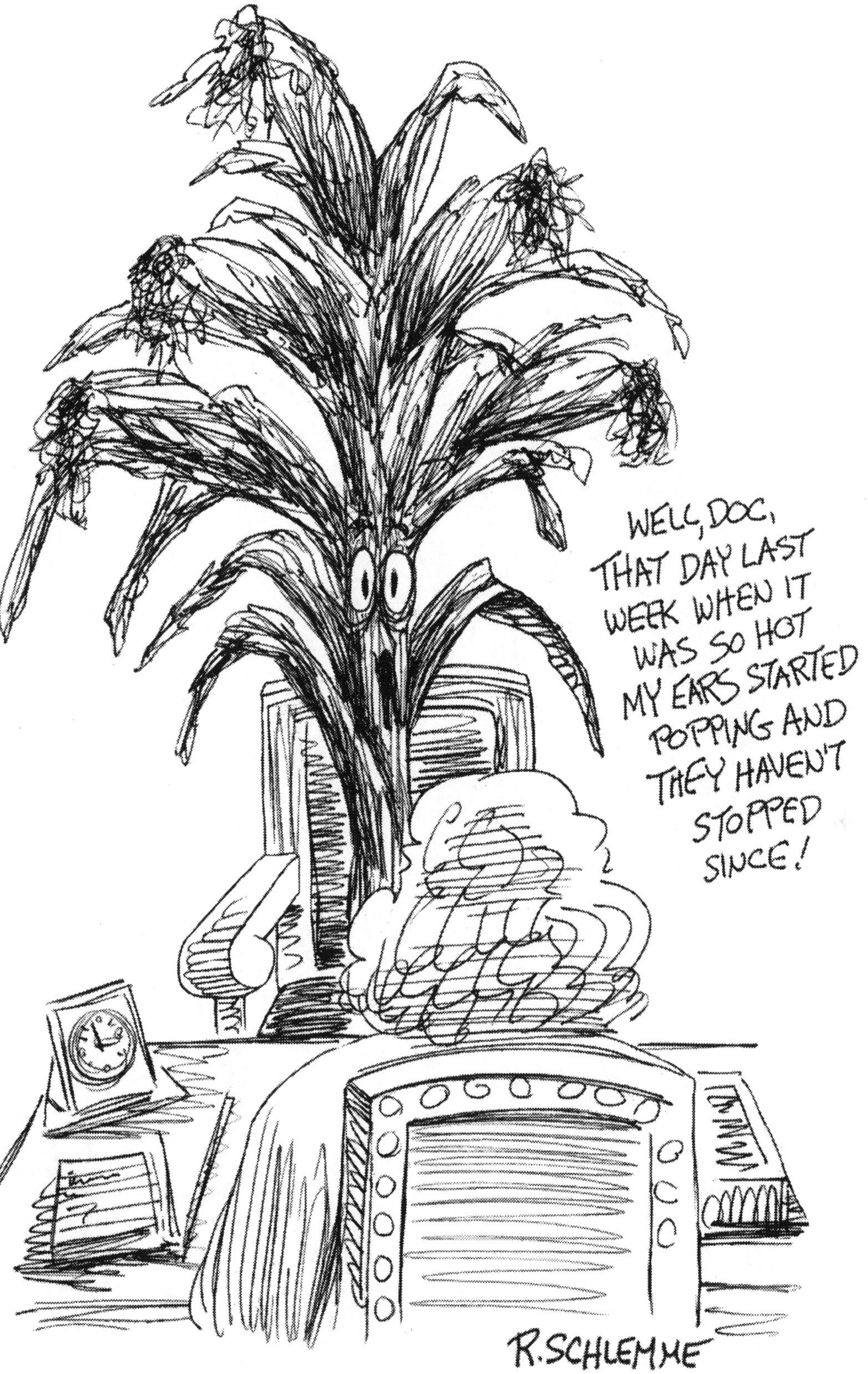
WELL, DOC, THAT DAY LAST WEEK WHEN IT WAS SO HOT MY EARS STARTED POPPING AND THEY HAVEN'T STOPPED SINCE!
R.SCHLEMME

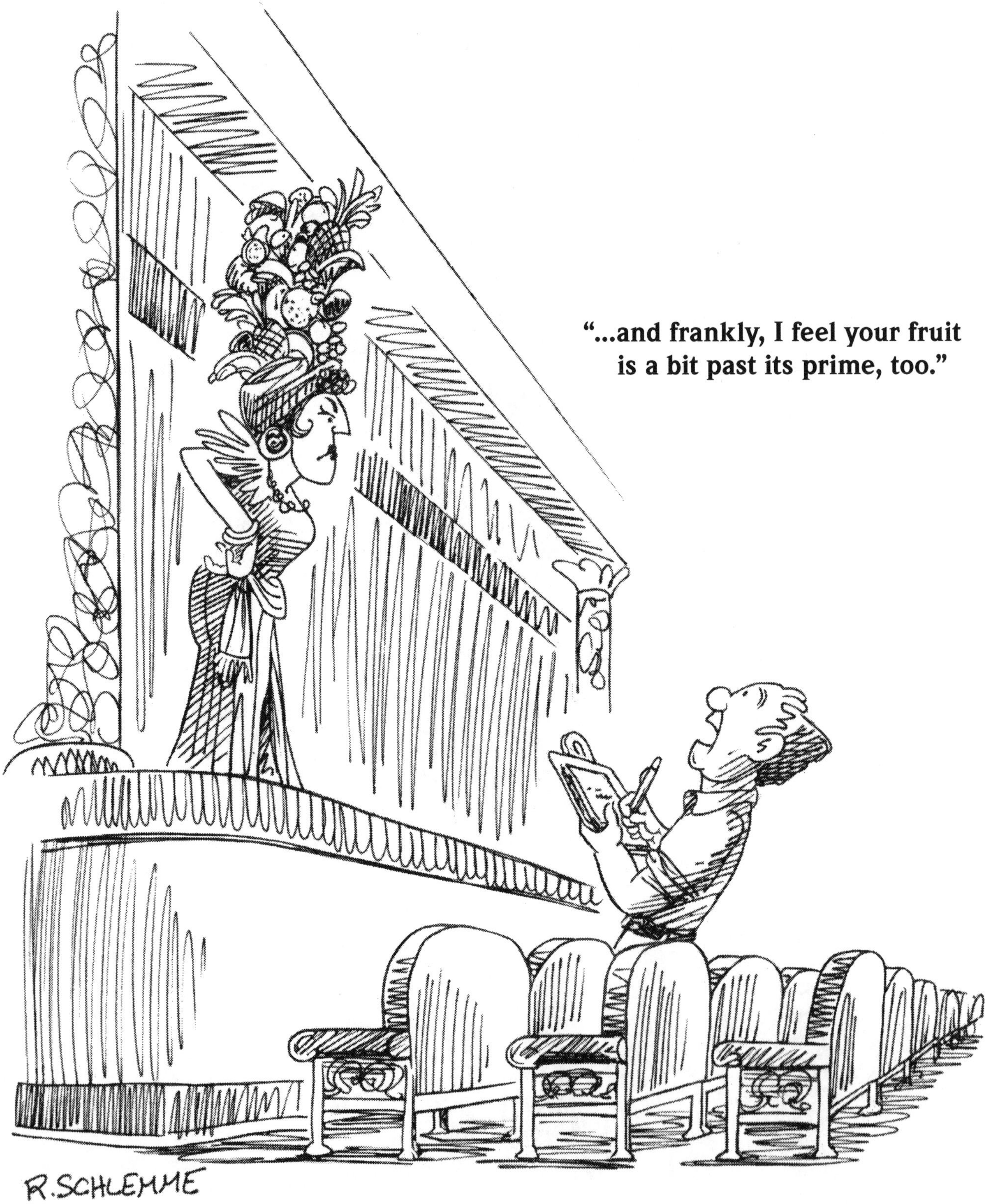
R.SCHLEMME

"...and frankly, I feel your fruit is a bit past its prime, too."

"Sorry! We don't handle 'small potatoes' loans."

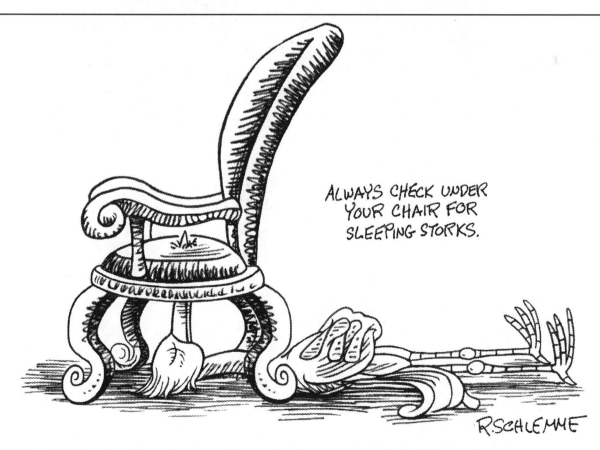

ALWAYS CHECK UNDER YOUR CHAIR FOR SLEEPING STORKS.

"I may be a paranoid schizophrenic but, at least, I'm a 'high-functioning' one."

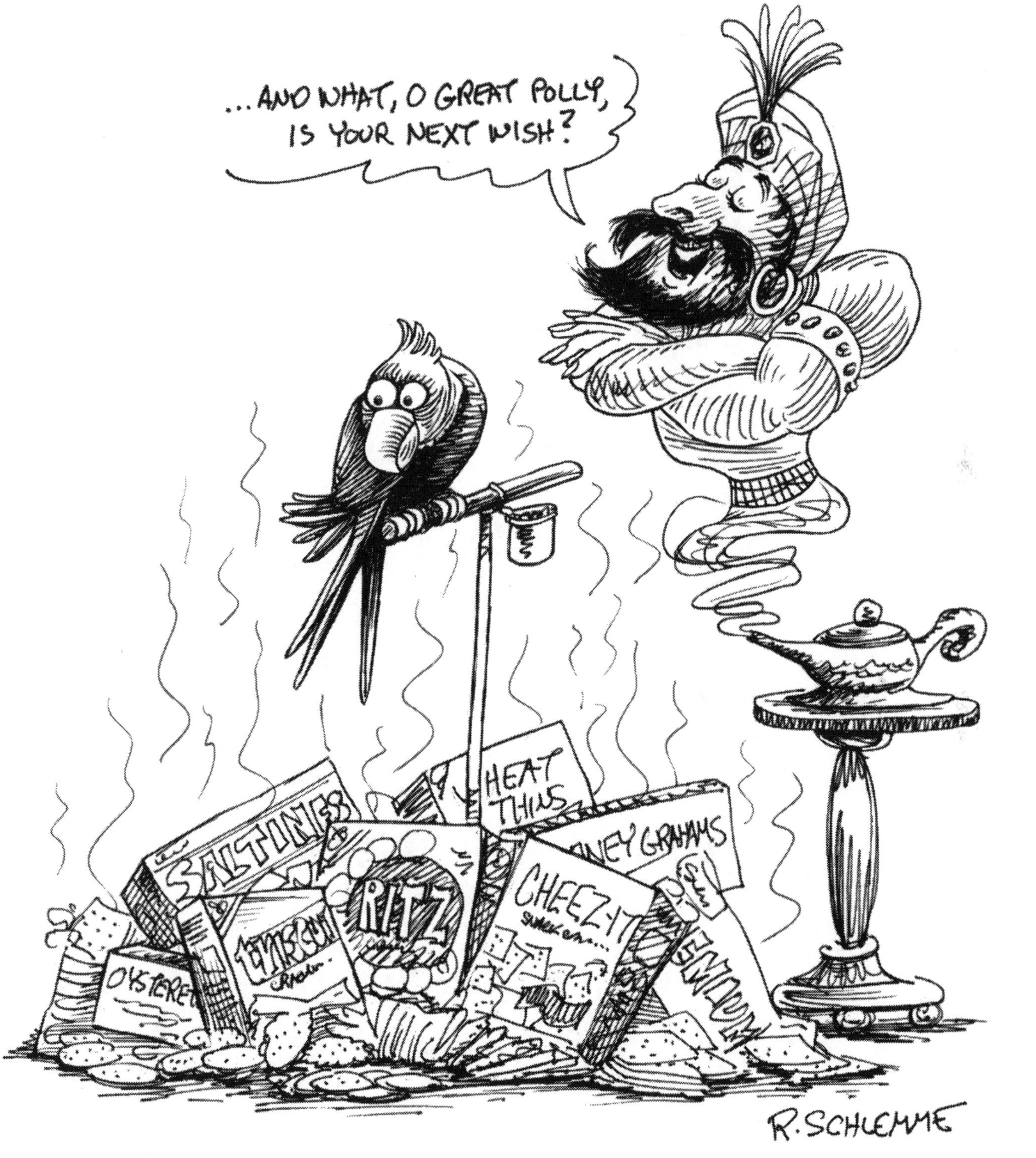
...AND WHAT, O GREAT POLLY,
IS YOUR NEXT WISH?
HEAT THINS
RITZ
CHEEZ-IT
R. SCHLEMME

"You're right...the flowers and feathers do compete."

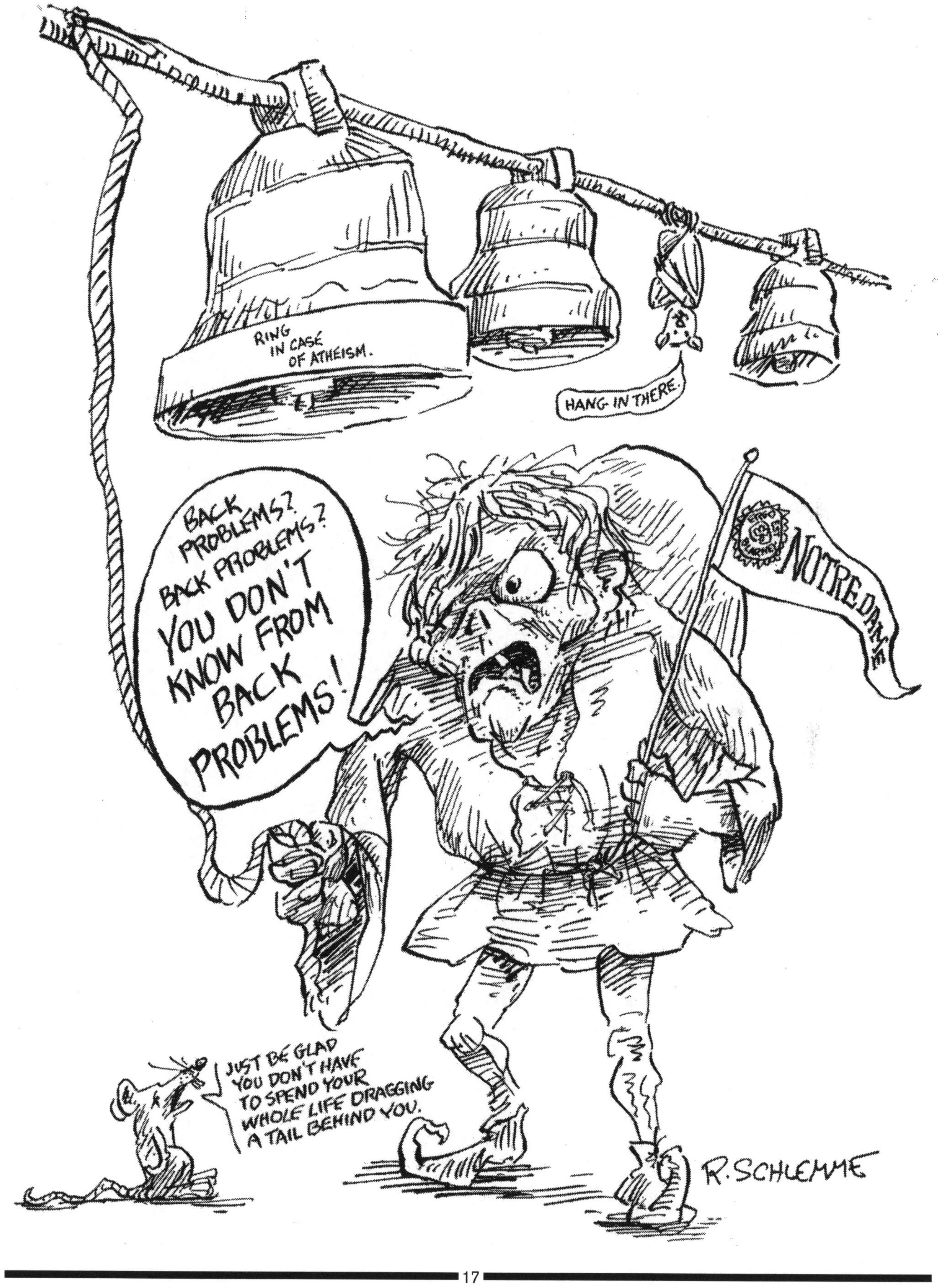
RING IN CASE OF ATHEISM.
HANG IN THERE.
BACK PROBLEMS? BACK PROBLEMS? YOU DON'T KNOW FROM BACK PROBLEMS!
NOTRE DAME
JUST BE GLAD YOU DON'T HAVE TO SPEND YOUR WHOLE LIFE DRAGGING A TAIL BEHIND YOU.
R. SCHLEMME

"Who tossed in my 'Barbie' doll?"

"The Ushers ignored a little crack like this
over at their place and look what happened."

"Winter solstice concerts leave me cold."

"Damn, Enos is still doin' it. Looks like they'll have to run another 'Find our box with the lucky noseberry in it' Contest again."

"Anybody think they can generate a good sidearm fastball today?"

"Wait'll she finds out he's a seedless."

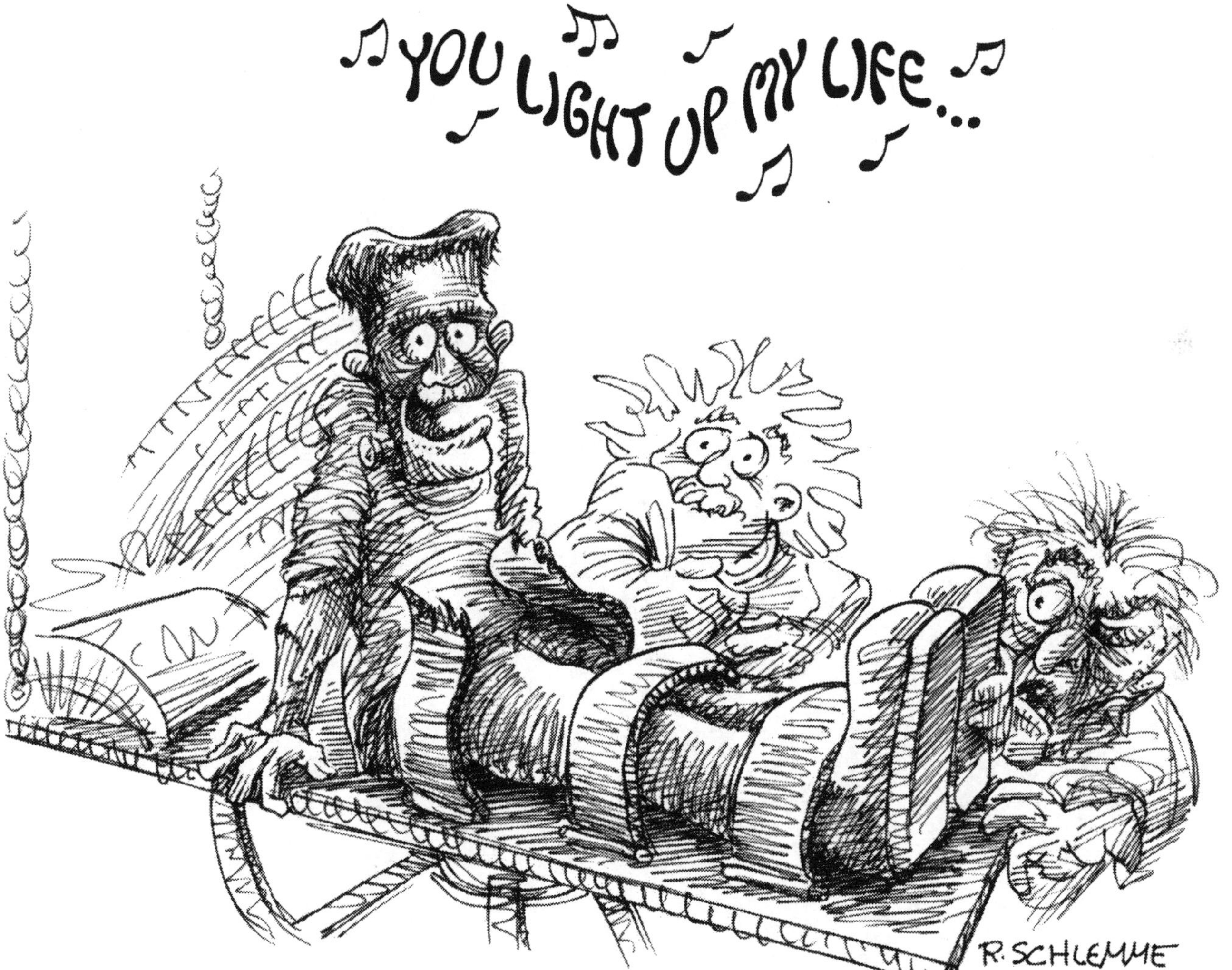
YOU LIGHT UP MY LIFE...
R. SCHLEMME

"I've always hated being
the last one to follow a trend."

R. SCHLEMME

"Make that 'To go'!
We're empire building!"

"I think it's seen one too many meteor showers."

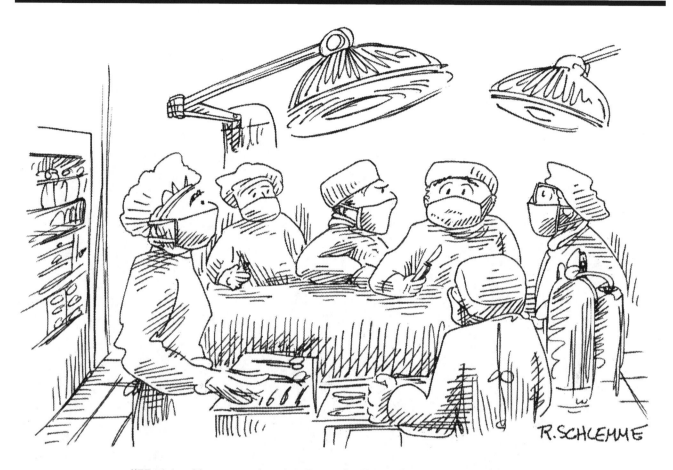

"Hold off, everybody, I can't find my lucky quarter."

"Tastes a touch seafoodish, but then, everything
down here tastes a touch seafoodish."

"Who called out to have a pall
cast over the occasion?"

"Taking our son along on your construction
job shouldn't have included using
him as your personal hardhat."

"What's so developmental about banging
little colored pegs with a big-ass mallet?"

"So, Jack, considering your solitary nature,
I suggest we bring in a helping hand
to get things turned around."

R.SCHLEMME

"Preferably something on your
terrace near the mosquitoes."

"You do any 'No-frills' flights?"

"Not a bad price once you know that
it includes hernia insurance coverage."

" *'Poetry on the go'* calling!"

"We know the wheel's rigged, but
still haven't figured out exactly how."

R.SCHLEMME

"Live with it, Sam! They're all at the cleaners!"

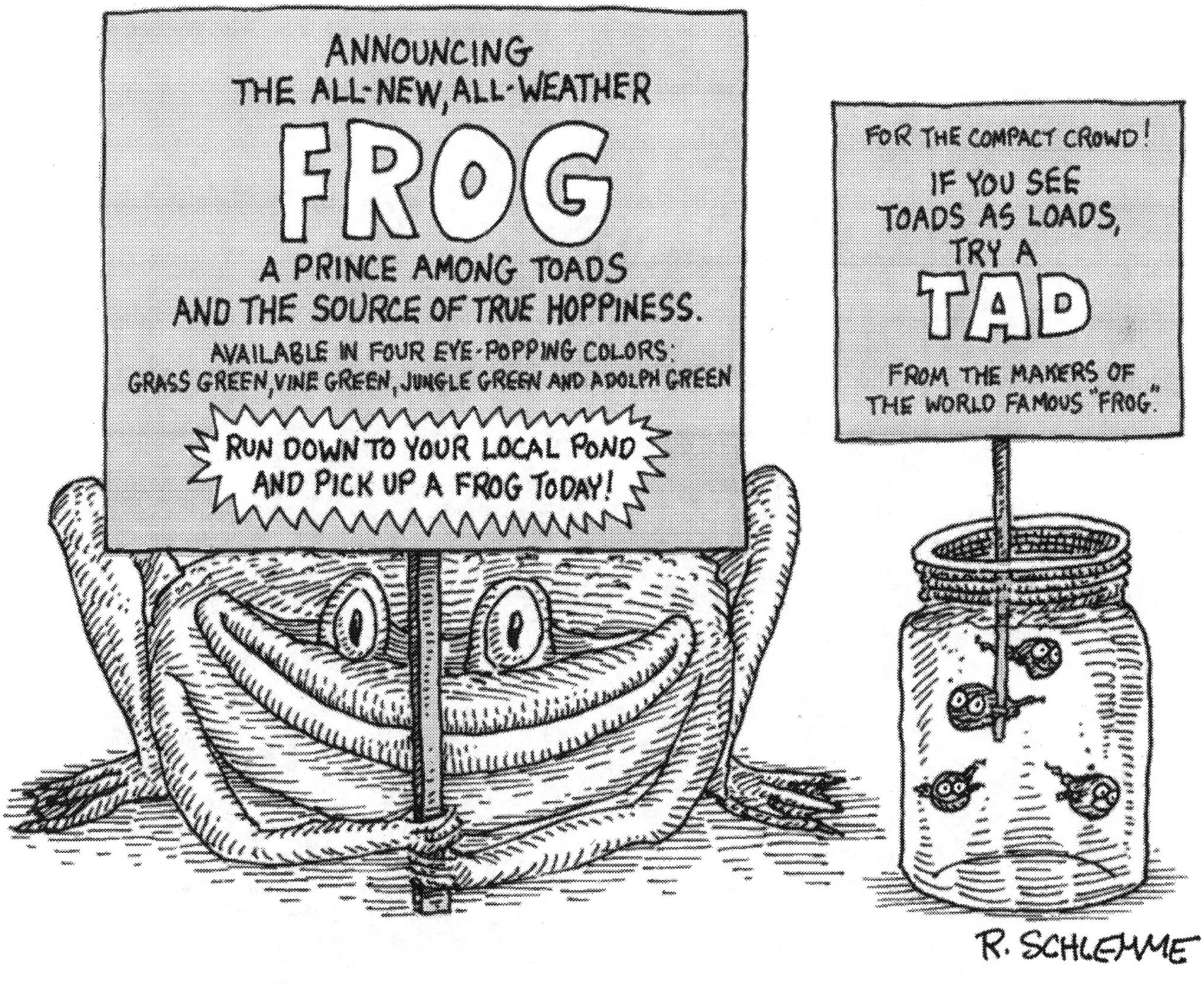
ANNOUNCING
THE ALL-NEW, ALL-WEATHER
FROG
A PRINCE AMONG TOADS
AND THE SOURCE OF TRUE HOPPINESS.
AVAILABLE IN FOUR EYE-POPPING COLORS:
GRASS GREEN, VINE GREEN, JUNGLE GREEN AND ADOLPH GREEN
RUN DOWN TO YOUR LOCAL POND
AND PICK UP A FROG TODAY!
FOR THE COMPACT CROWD!
IF YOU SEE
TOADS AS LOADS,
TRY A
TAD
FROM THE MAKERS OF
THE WORLD FAMOUS "FROG."
R. SCHLEMME

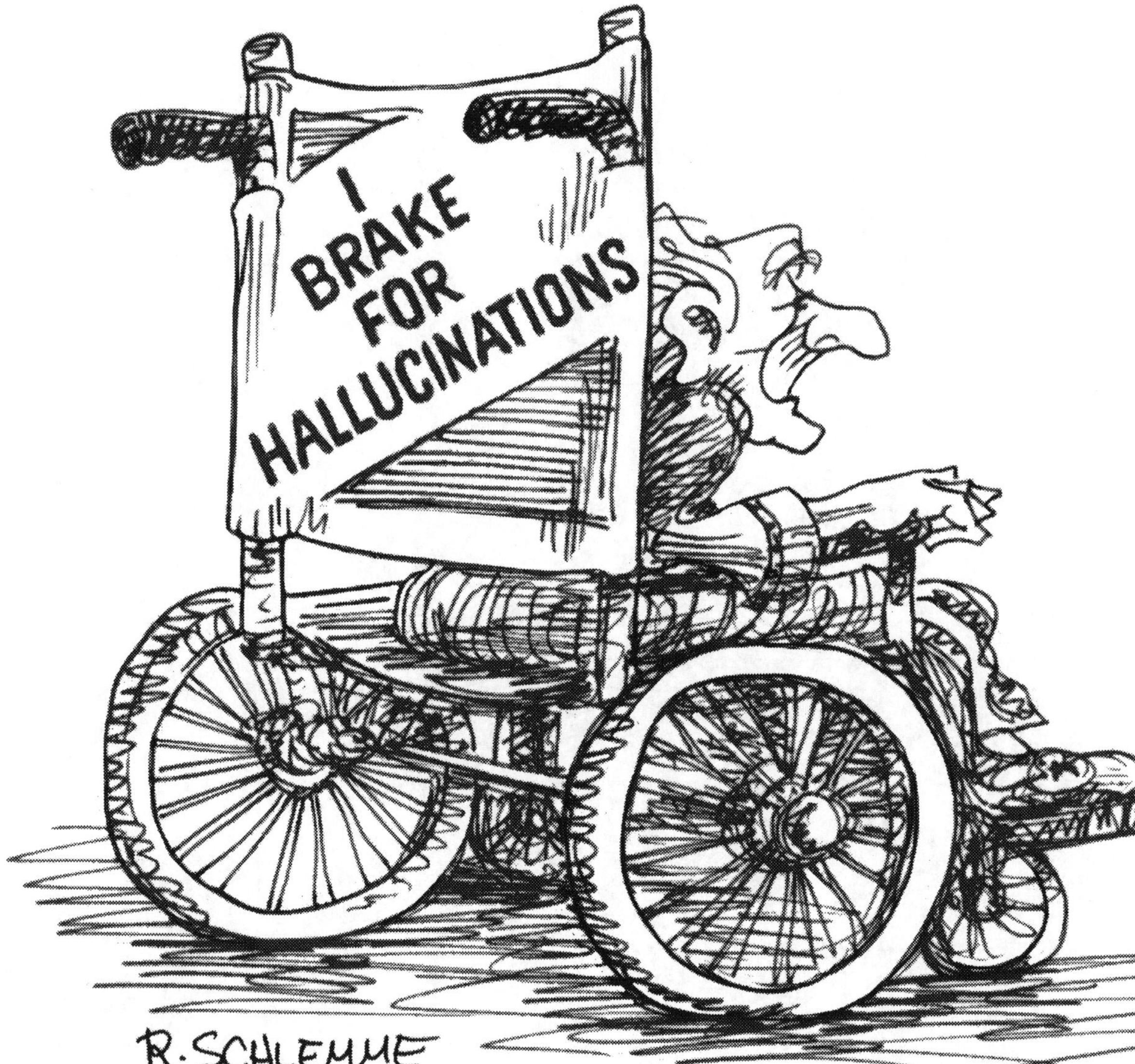
I BRAKE FOR HALLUCINATIONS
R. SCHLEMME

"He still confuses *'Sit, Rex!'*
with *'Get a death grip on the
speaker's closest limb!'*."

"I'll bet you forgot to say *'Piddy-widdy Puss-puss'* before trying to pet her."

"OK, Foxy! Come out with those hens up!"

"The real miracle would be his getting away
in one piece if they read the scam."

"Sure, it's a little awkward, but I haven't had
any hunters target me since I began wearing it."

"Obviously, you're someone who knows how to make a funnel stylish."

R. SCHLEMME

R. SCHLEMME

"Surprise! How do you like
our new clam-spring chair?"

Shady character.

R. SCHLEMME

"Hold off! Caesar just
ducked out to hit the john."

"I can see why the kennel wants
them to go as a sibling group."

"Just how much longer do we continue
to indulge our daughter's flights of fancy?"

"Before we begin, does anyone feel unduly
anxious about doing these exercises?"

R. SCHLEMME

Which remote actually turns on the TV?

"I just forgot what
it's supposed to say."

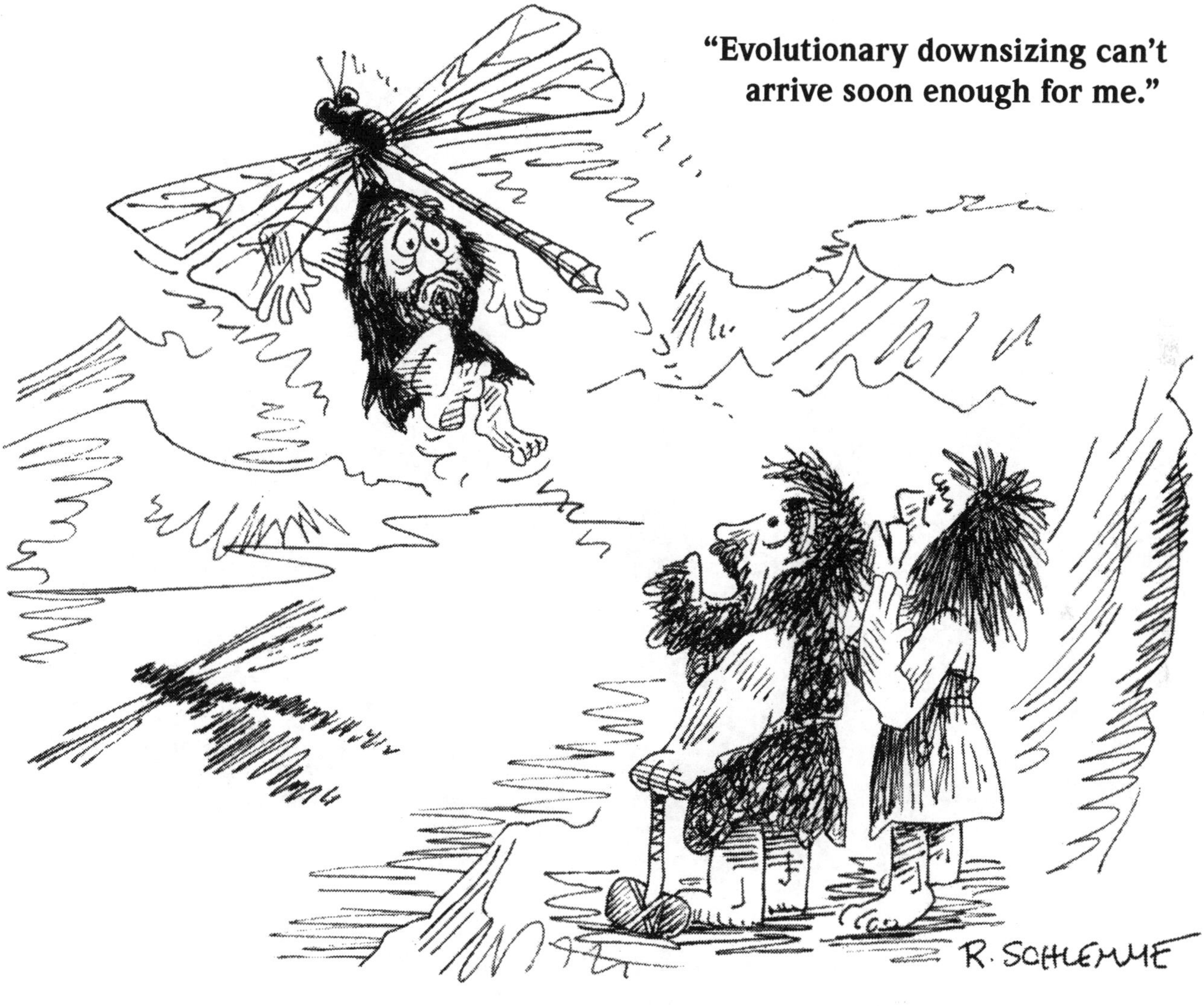
R. SCHLEMME

"Evolutionary downsizing can't arrive soon enough for me."

"...and as for the news releases, do you
prefer the traditional 'Jeanne d'Arc' or
a more trendy 'Joan of Arc'?"

"I'm heading back.
There's no tartar sauce."

"See, I told you how well-marked
all the roads in Britain are!"

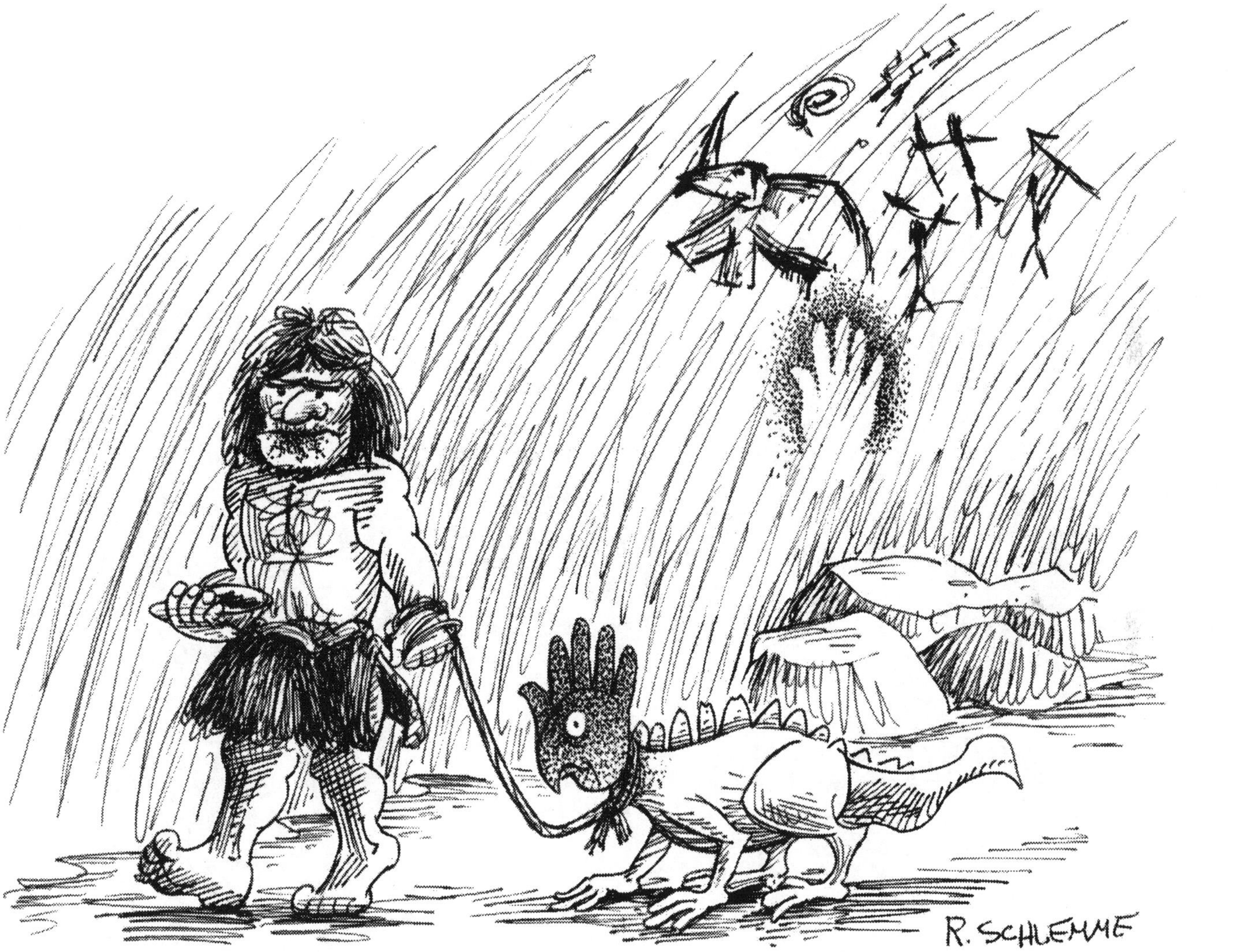
R. SCHLEMME

"Offering anything that skitters?"

R.SCHLEMME

"I've never enjoyed commuting."

"I know mine's a minority opinion but, I'm still betting on a non-evolving universe."

"I feel a great big bear hug comin' on."

"Beep-beep, deadass!"

**"It won't sell unless it spells
out something obscene."**

"Like many creative types, Gino constantly searches for new challenges in his life."

R. SCHLEMME

**"It's not a total cure but increasing
your water intake should help considerably."**

"Hmmm...Still nothing open in The Queen's Chamber.
Looks like you're stuck with aphid-milking a bit longer."

"Either of you guys seen our
new kid since the last break?"

"Sure we're family, but I still feel
uneasy doing these muzzle-to-muzzles."

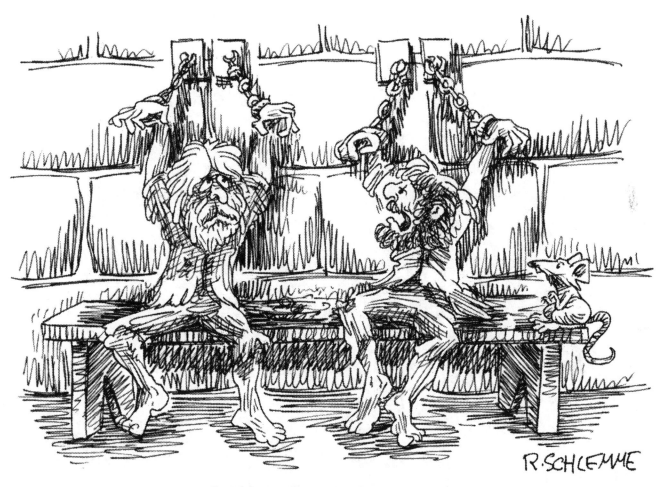

"...even worse, I think all my
credit cards have begun triggering
late-payment penalties."

"Will the slayer of a large blue-green dragon
parked at the cave's entrance please move it.
It's blocking our 'Free the Virgin Princess' parade."

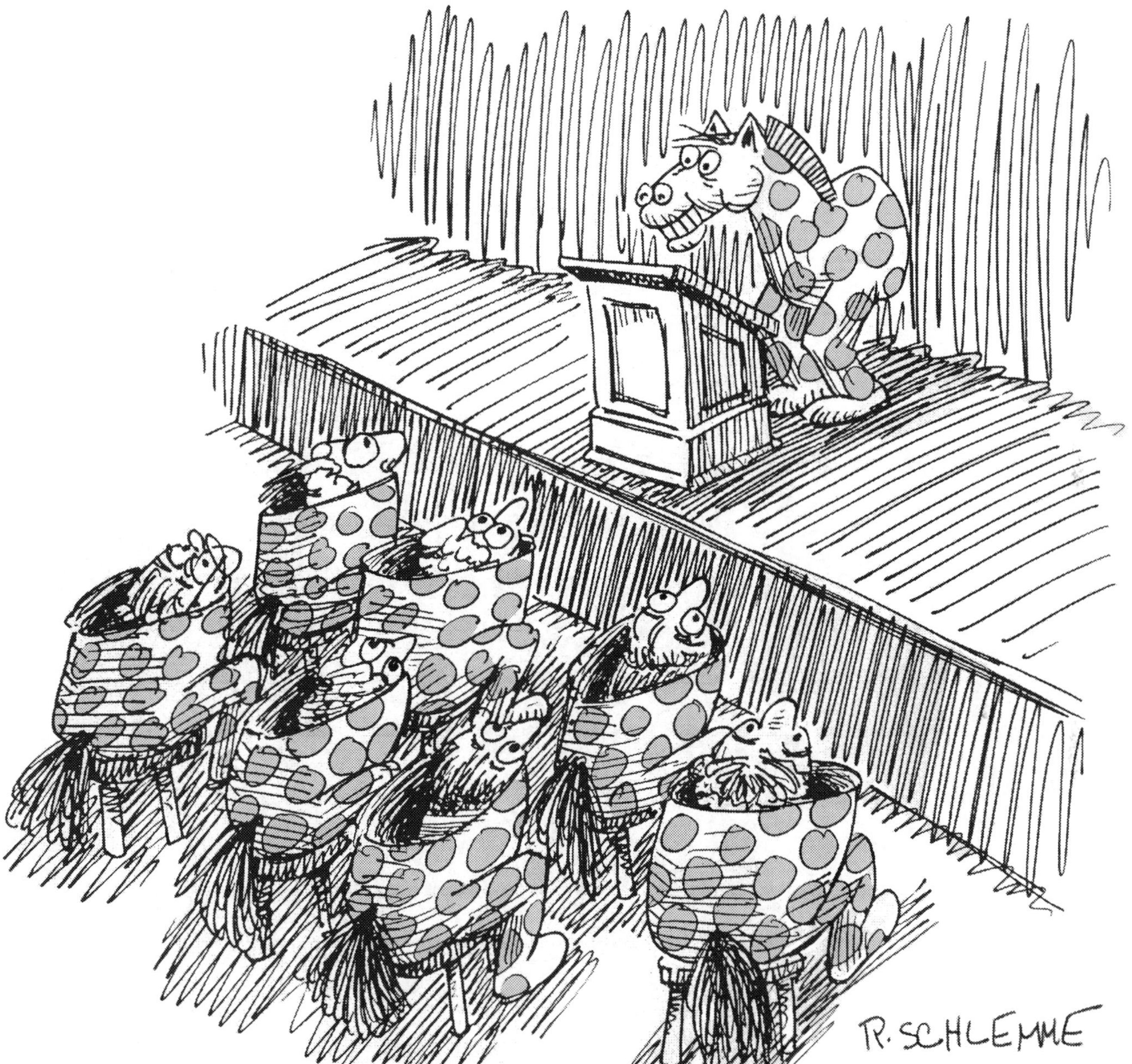
R. SCHLEMME

Leadership Seminar.

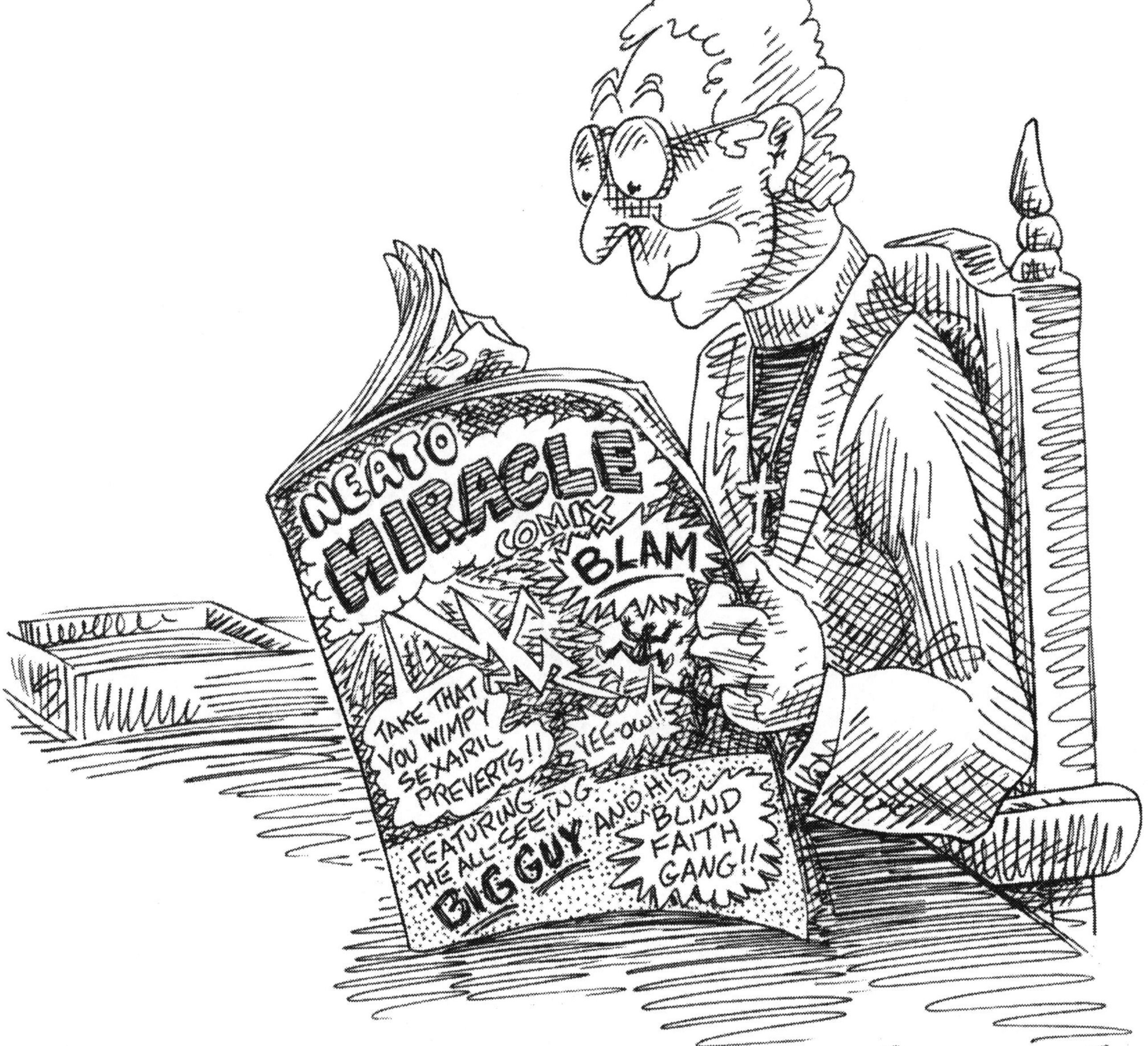
NEATO
MIRACLE
COMIX
BLAM
TAKE THAT YOU WIMPY SEXARIL PREVERTS!!
YEE-OW!!
FEATURING THE ALL-SEEING BIG GUY AND HIS BLIND FAITH GANG!!
R. SCHLEMME

"Lower it a touch and we can go for a new personal best in The Dog Leash High Jump."

"Thanks again, everyone! His Majesty just concluded that 'more' is definately not 'merrier'!"

"What a great hand! Hopefully, you'll show
equal enthusiasm for our keynote speaker once
I finish testing the mike's sound level."

PALEOLITHIC 'ARMS' MARKETING

R. SCHLEMME

**"Elegantly engineered by nature and, when
launched at the proper velocity, guaranteed
to neutralize one's opponent instantly."**

"I keep getting this odd feeling that
we're actually a ménage à trois."

"Holding any unclaimed Christmas cards?"

"I was always led to believe
that writer's block appears a bit
later in the creative process."

"Drop as a well-disciplined unit...
and that's an order!"

The Great Donut Massacre.

R.SCHLEMME

R.SCHLEMME

"Leaners seldom achieve best-seller status."

"From now on, check every applicant
for gas cooking experience."

"I've got this spooky feeling that
before we get very far, somebody's
gonna want a piece of us."

"Once upon a time there lived a genetically lucky
royal couple whose incredibly long life span
landed them in The Guinness Book of Records."

Captionless!

To paraphrase the well-known quote,
'A cartoon minus verbiage (if well thought
out) can also be worth a thousand words'.
Hopefully, this double-page spread
clearly illustrates the point.

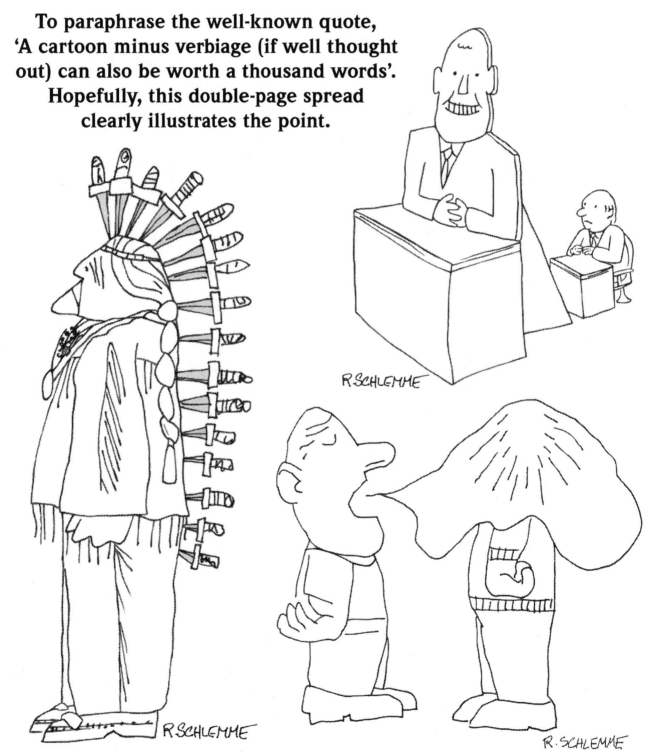

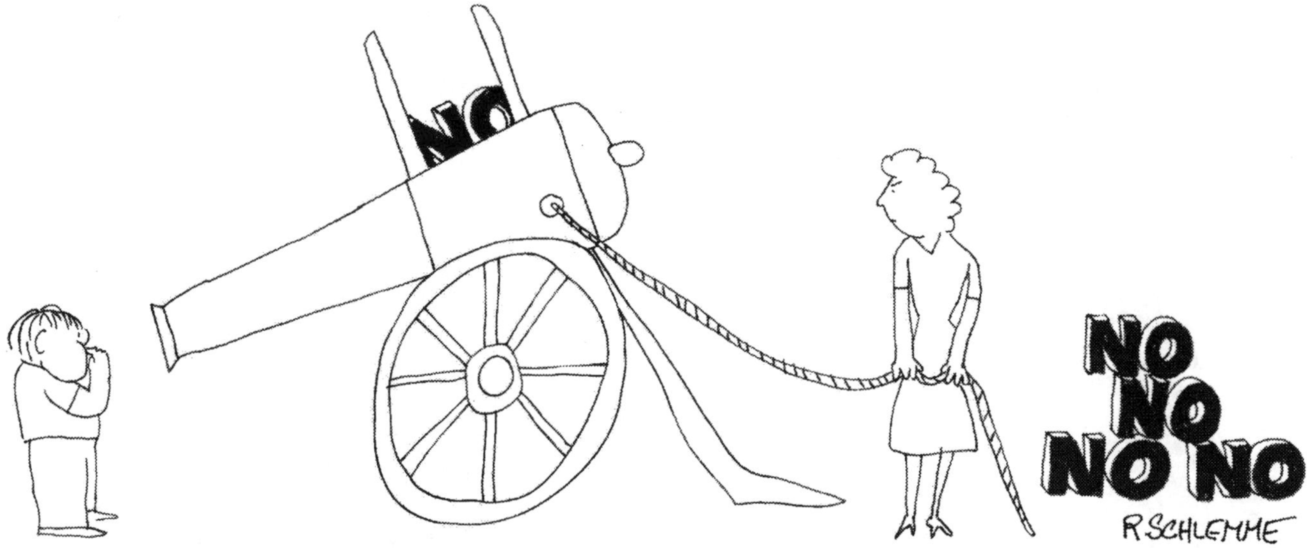
NO
NO
NO
NO NO
R.SCHLEMME

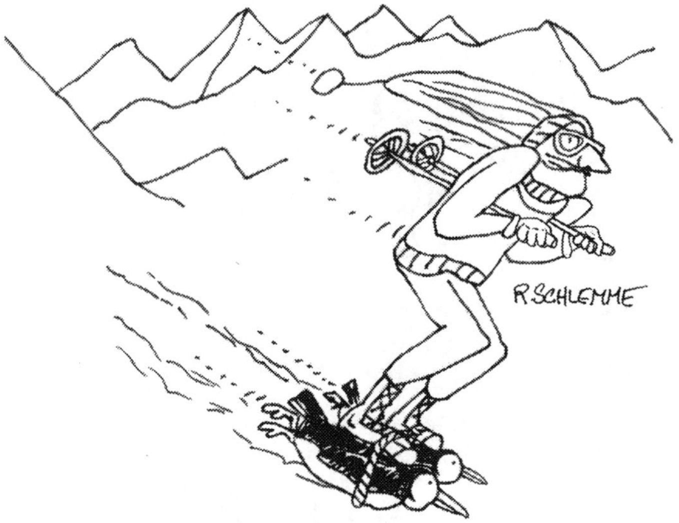
R.SCHLEMME

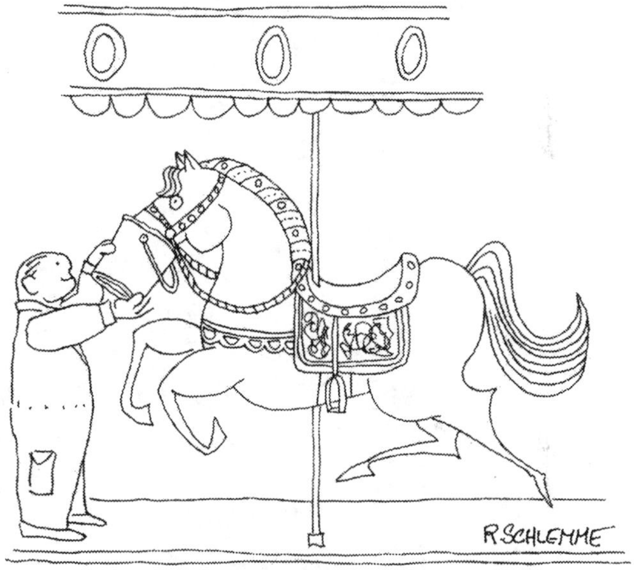
R.SCHLEMME

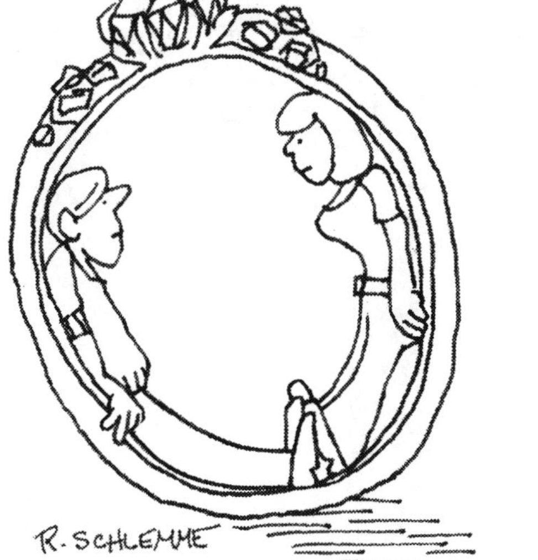
R.SCHLEMME

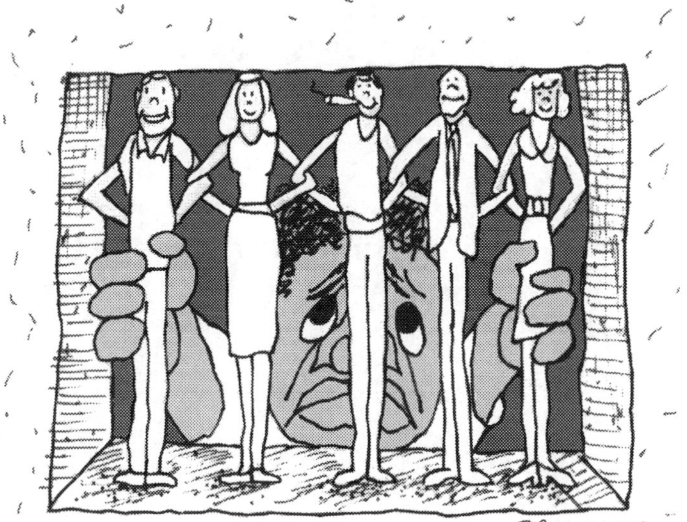
R.SCHLEMME

"Anything on the menu that still looks
visually appetizing as it's being digested?"

"So much for teaching
a pet to do my signature."

Shakespeare in the Park

R. SCHLEMME

"I see you talked
Cousin Claude into taking
a flying leap again."

R. SCHLEMME

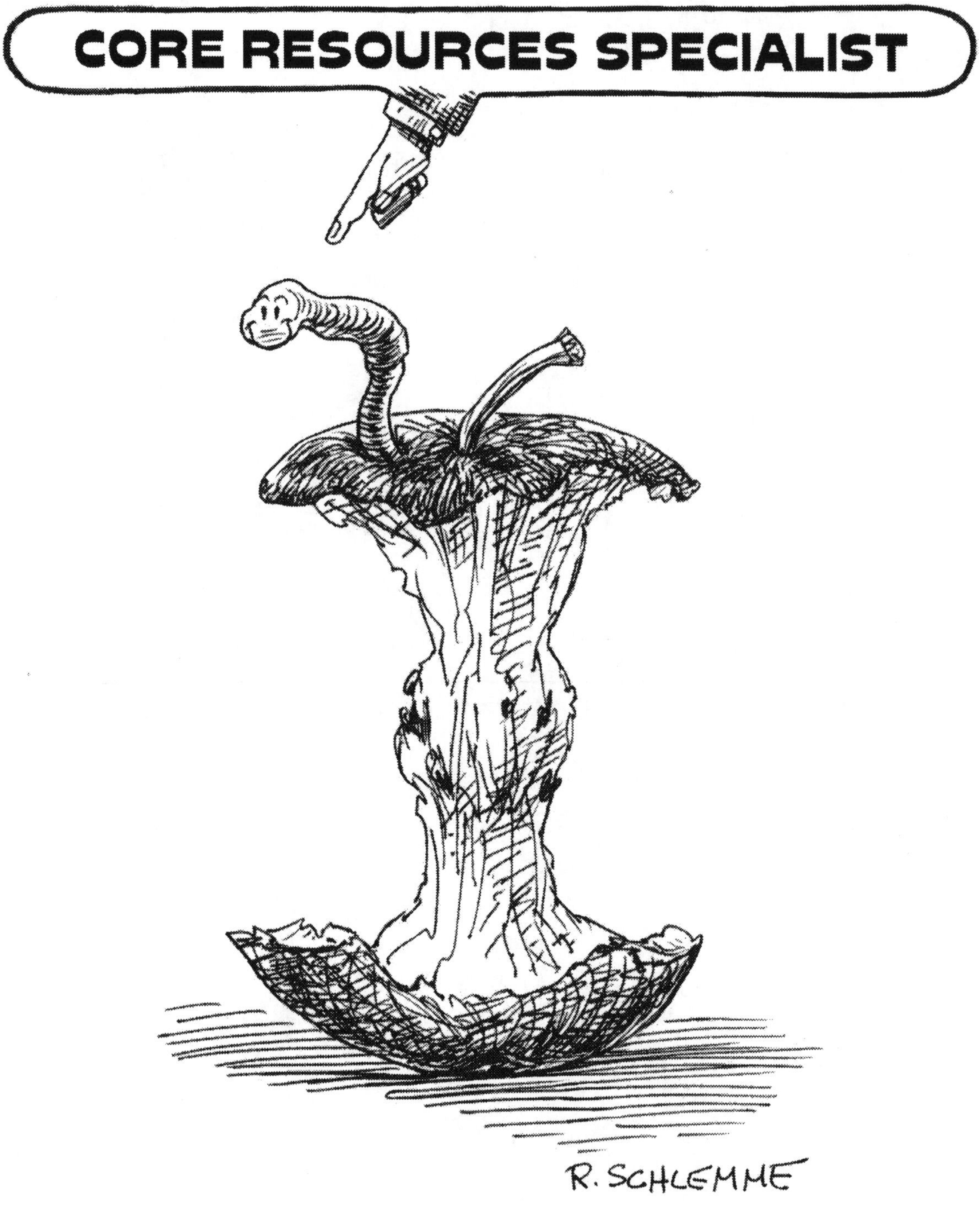
CORE RESOURCES SPECIALIST
R. SCHLEMME

"Besides getting Willie some extra break time, it provides cheap baggage carousel amusement for the passengers still waiting around upstairs."

"Wow! That was our cleanest
plank walker entry ever!"

"...then there's the off chance that you're
just not a 'Giorgio Armani' kind of guy."

**Bemedaled
military heroes generally
(as well as admirally)
list to port.**

R. SCHLEMME

"Stowaway! Stowaway!"

R. SCHLEMME

"Hold off, guys! Three of you personal demons
will have to take the next one."

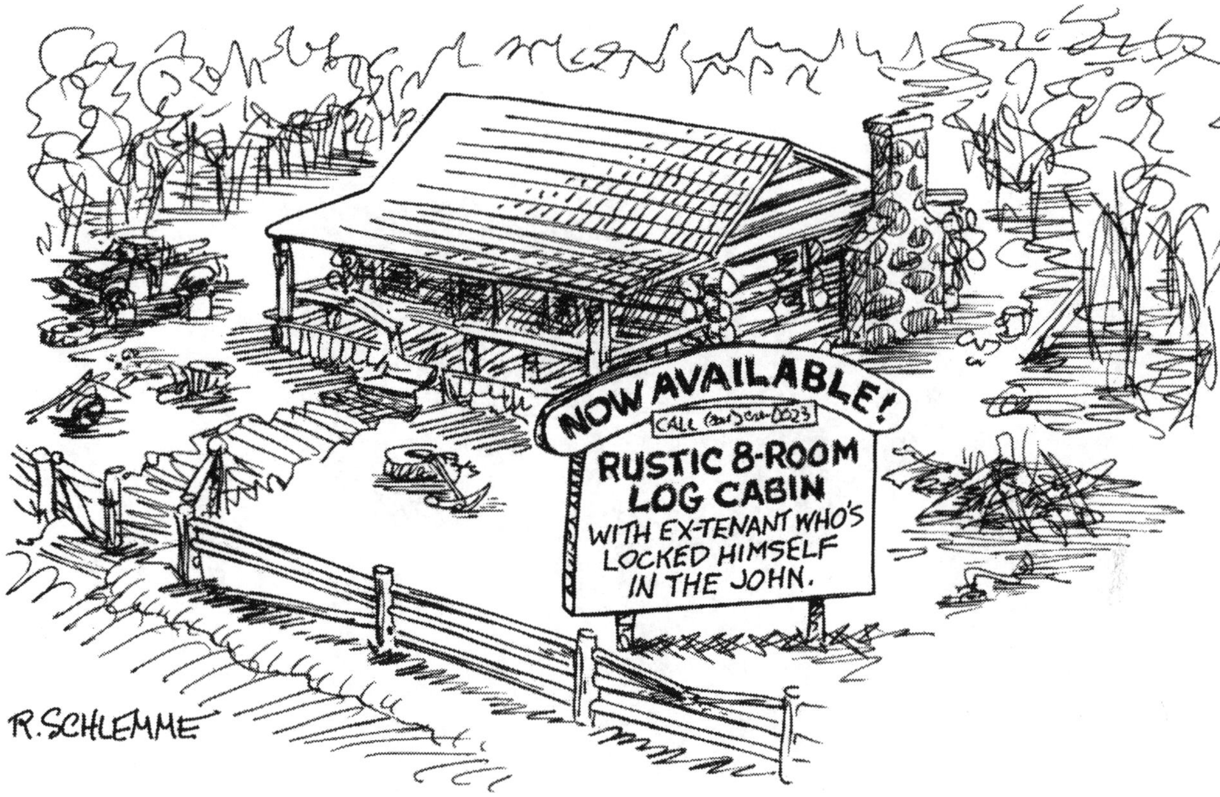
NOW AVAILABLE!
RUSTIC 8-ROOM
LOG CABIN
WITH EX-TENANT WHO'S
LOCKED HIMSELF
IN THE JOHN.
R.SCHLEMME

THE BEST OF BOTH WORLDS

R. SCHLEMME

"If you'd stayed on that diet,
this probably wouldn't have happened."

A CONSEQUENCE OF UNHEEDED WARNINGS.

HOW TO MAKE JOUSTING TEDIOUS.

"...Clause 21, Section C. In the event of any major damage to armor, related equipment or steed, the aforementioned victor retains unlimited right to petition his opponent for full reimbursement within..."

"I just gave at the orifice."

"I think The Great Gabardini should consider a less boastful adjective."

"Nothing personal but I've decided to give stern public warnings a shot."

"Maybe something. Maybe nothing. Probably nothing."

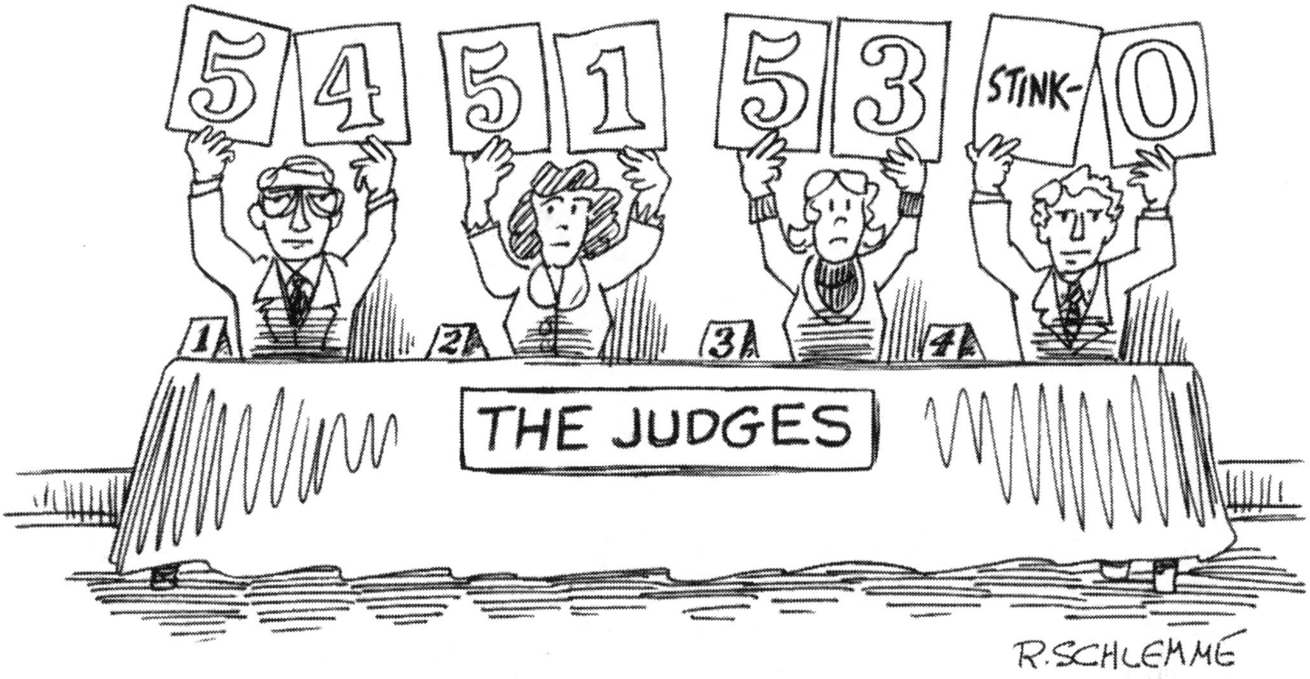
5
4
5
1
5
3
STINK-
0
1
2
3
4
THE JUDGES
R. SCHLEMME

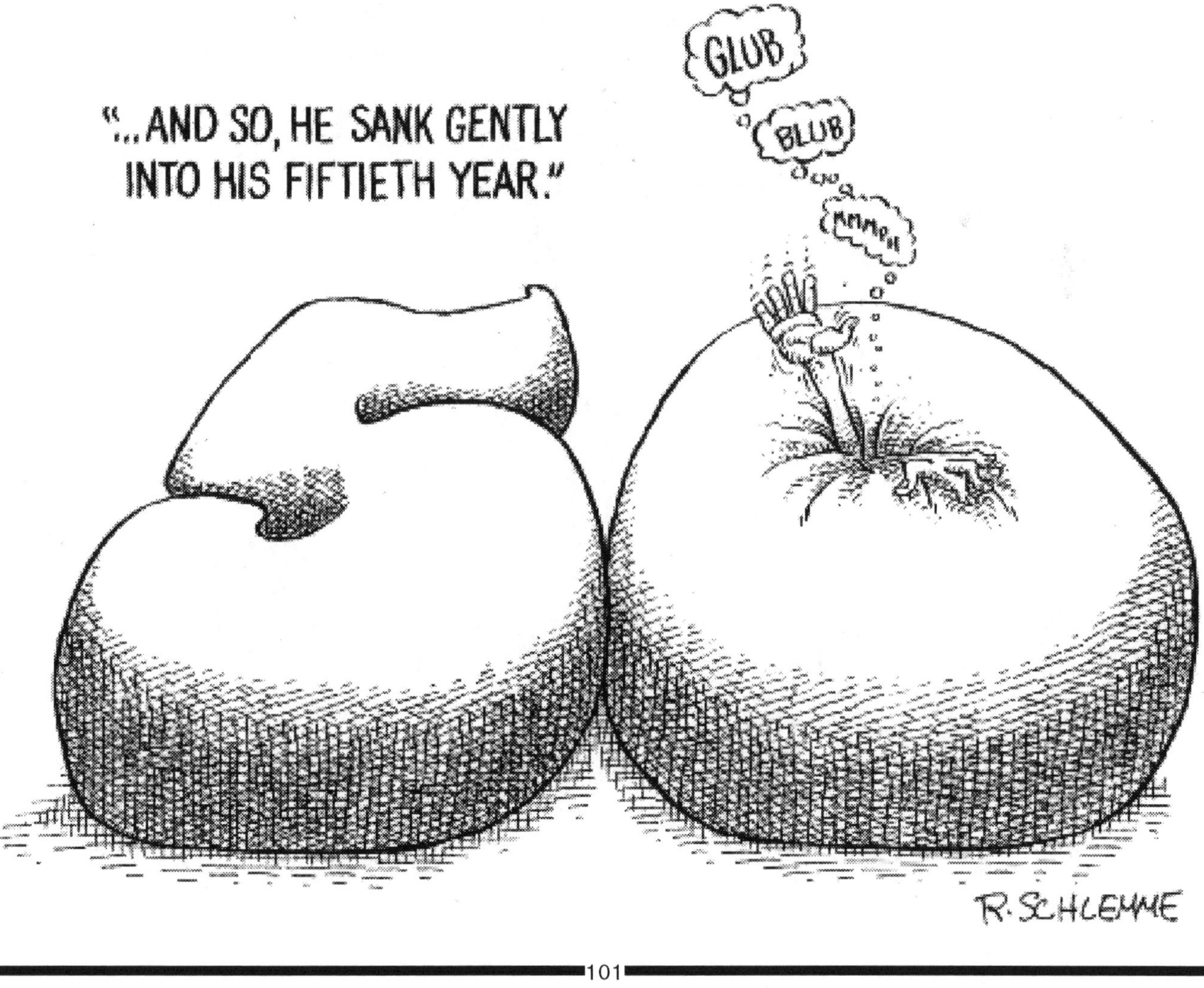
"...AND SO, HE SANK GENTLY INTO HIS FIFTIETH YEAR."
GLUB
BLUB
R. SCHLEMME

"I find it a definatively elegant statement, Renaissance-wise."

R. SCHLEMME

"Hello, police...I want to report
a big racquet being made next door."

"I often wonder how parents coped before Baby-Stay Tape."

R. SCHLEMME

"Great fit! Got it in any
really garish colors?"

R.SCHLEMME

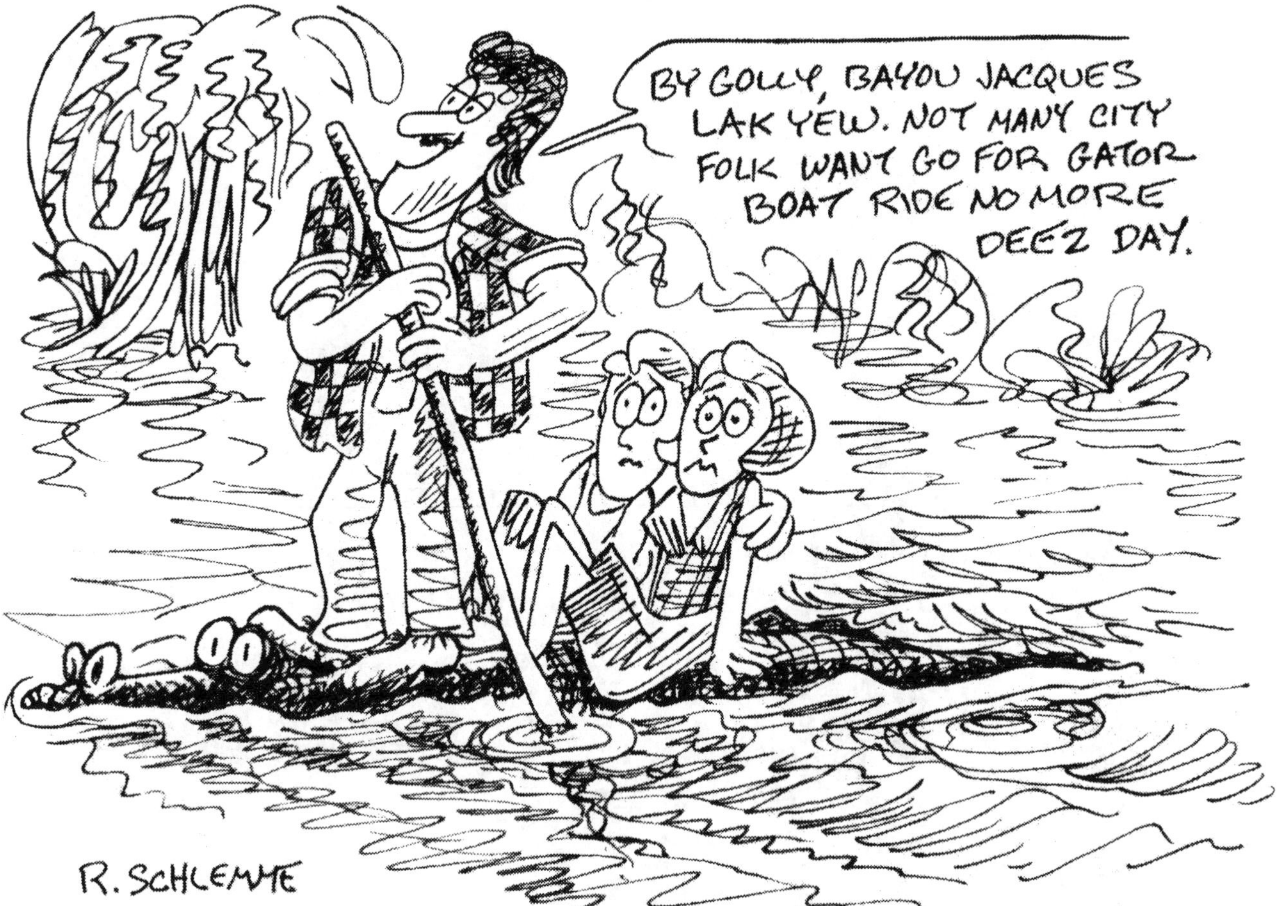
BY GOLLY, BAYOU JACQUES LAK YEW. NOT MANY CITY FOLK WANT GO FOR GATOR BOAT RIDE NO MORE DEEZ DAY.
R. SCHLEMME

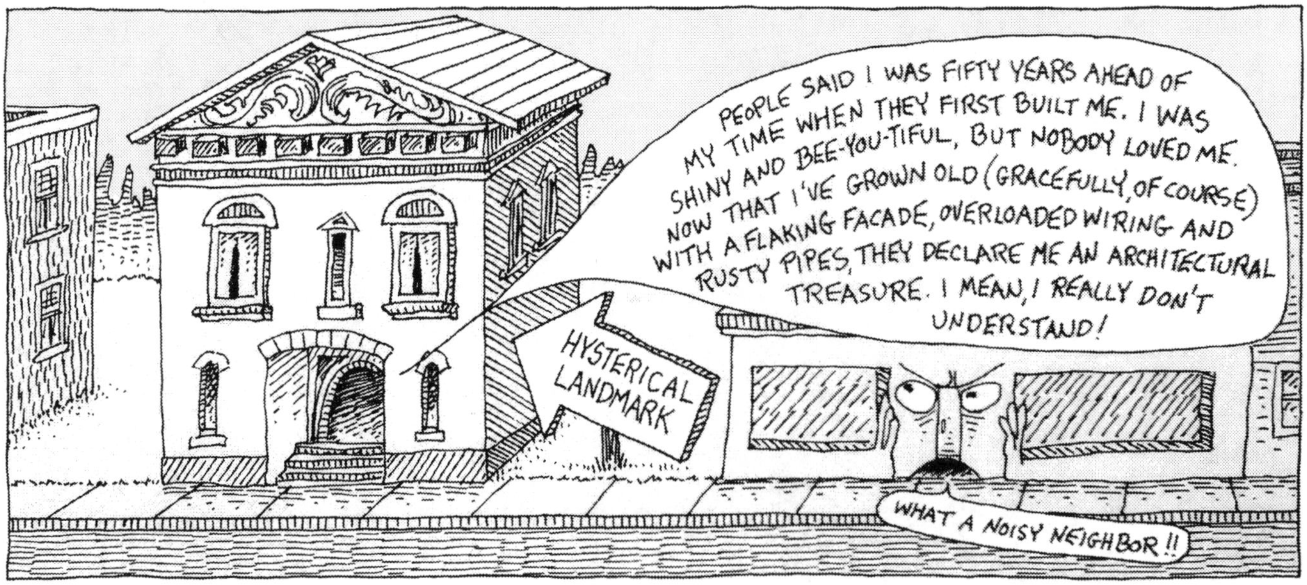
PEOPLE SAID I WAS FIFTY YEARS AHEAD OF MY TIME WHEN THEY FIRST BUILT ME. I WAS SHINY AND BEE-YOU-TIFUL, BUT NOBODY LOVED ME. NOW THAT I'VE GROWN OLD (GRACEFULLY, OF COURSE) WITH A FLAKING FACADE, OVERLOADED WIRING AND RUSTY PIPES, THEY DECLARE ME AN ARCHITECTURAL TREASURE. I MEAN, I REALLY DON'T UNDERSTAND!
HYSTERICAL LANDMARK
WHAT A NOISY NEIGHBOR!!

R.SCHLEMME

"Unfortunately, sir, a total
lack of art skills really
doesn't qualify you."

"I'd really like to have those barrel elevations raised
a touch prior to my upcoming walk-by review."

"First time up, eh, kid?"

R. SCHLEMME

"It's always real special comin' out here over the holidays tuh unwind and wonder why my stock portfolio tanked another 40% this year."

KNIVES
& BLADES
SHARPENED
WHILE·U·WAIT

R·SCHLEMMÉ

"As I see it Ms. Dumpty, his
injuries from the fall concern me far less
than his high cholesterol readings."

R. SCHLEMME

"Thinking Summer vacation season already?"

"My parents' fervent wish was that I choose
a career where everyone would look up to me."

"I've called our meeting to discuss a nasty
corporate manipulation rumor going around."

"I hereby declare me
The King of String."

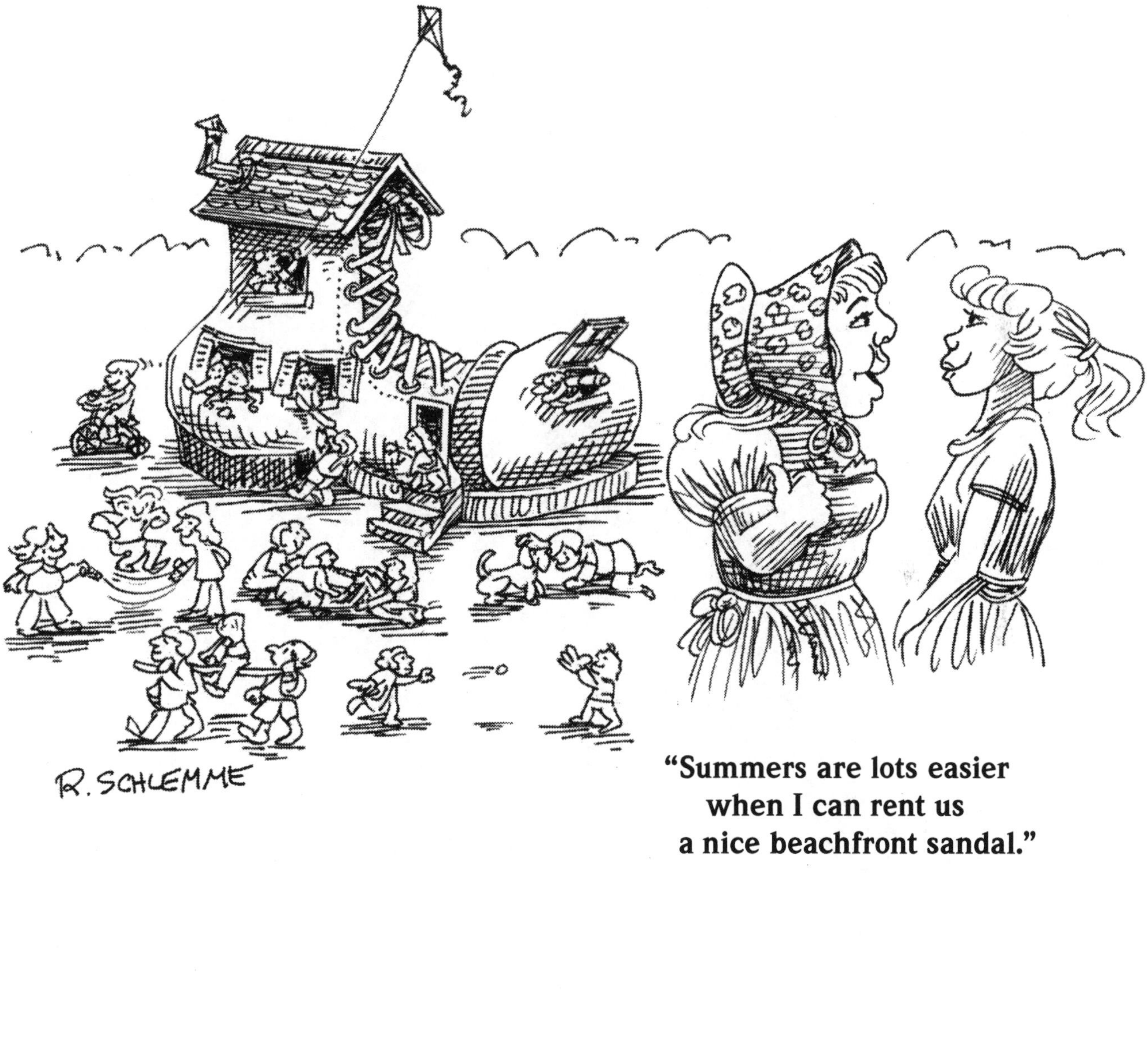
R. SCHLEMME

"Summers are lots easier when I can rent us a nice beachfront sandal."

"Getting ahead and moving up...
both problems solved."

R.SCHLEMME

"Alert the royal household. I'm leaning
toward resplendent for tomorrow."

R. SCHLEMME

"You move with the natural ease of someone comfortable in their blobbiness."

"Like Frost, I too, often prefer the road less traveled."

"I simply love what you've done
with your pumice and schist."

At The Live Ammo Convention.

R. SCHLEMME

"Your Dud Club
meeting's over there!"

"Hey, doc! I'll bet you never request
him to 'inhale deeply' again!"

"I've got three anti-inflammatories and
a pair of transplant rejection surpressors."

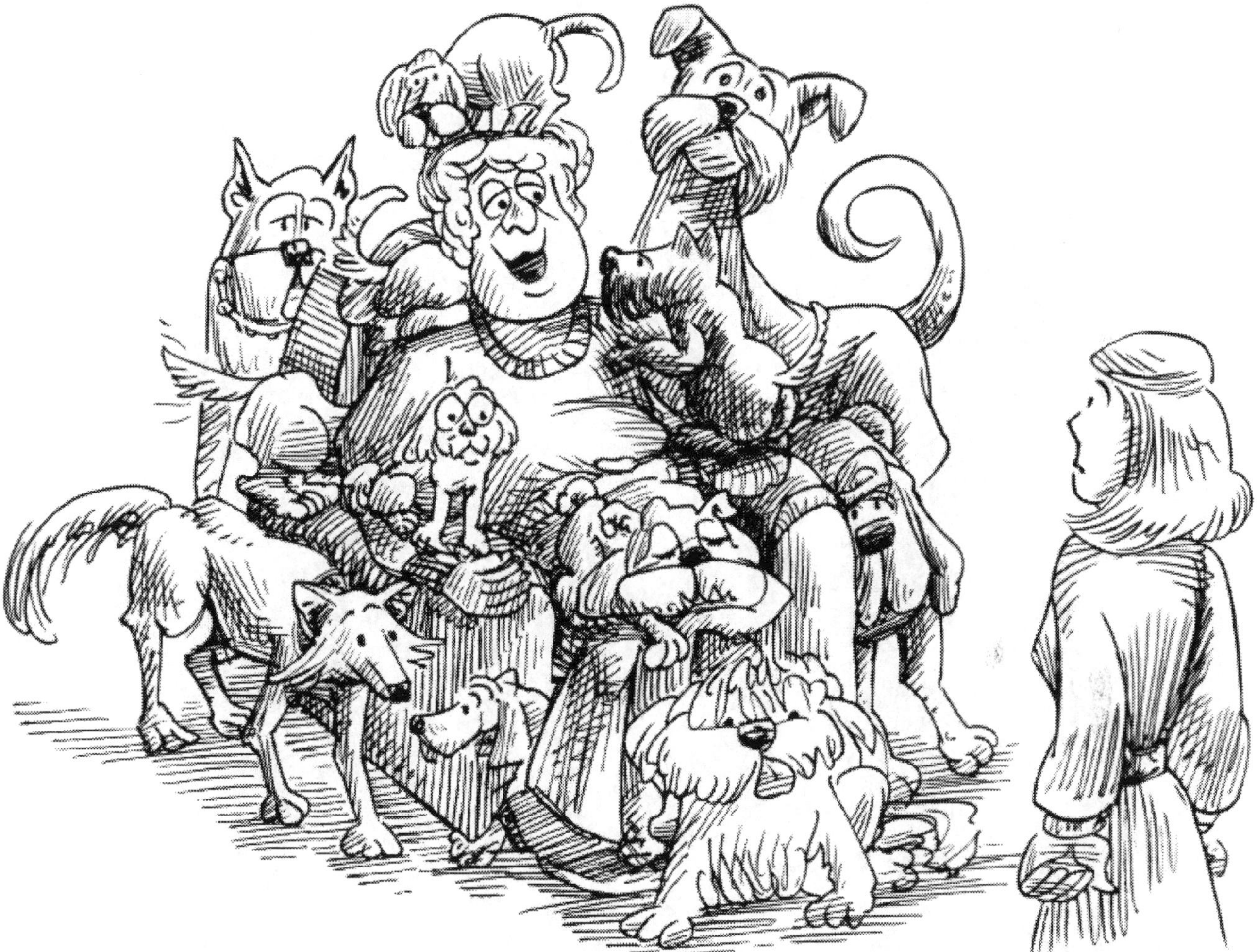
R.SCHLEMME

"It's good to be a god!"

**Dress for success
in chess.**

R. SCHLEMME

"No voice-activated responses!
No spectacular visual surprises!
No sonic bells and whistles!
How totally Dark Ages!"

BAD AT MANAGING LUMP SUM LOTTO WINNINGS.

"I suspect that paranoia resides up there."

R. SCHLEMME

**"Play their national anthem!
Play their national anthem!"**

"I forgot my pin number again."

R. SCHLEMME

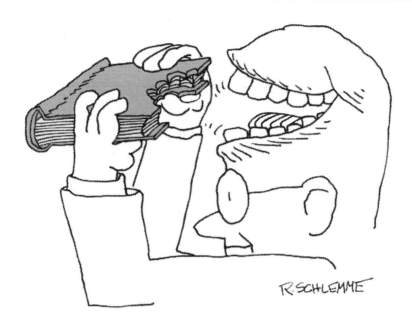

R. SCHLEMME

Still hungry?

**Now that you've gone thru Roy Schlemme's
latest collection of unconventional visuals
(hopefully, with a good impression) and
find yourself wanting a little more, be
of good cheer. His seven previous
soft-cover paperbacks all remain
available from AuthorHouse.
For a little look at them,
check the back cover.**

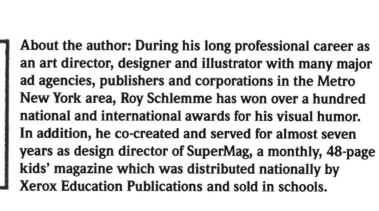

About the author: During his long professional career as an art director, designer and illustrator with many major ad agencies, publishers and corporations in the Metro New York area, Roy Schlemme has won over a hundred national and international awards for his visual humor. In addition, he co-created and served for almost seven years as design director of SuperMag, a monthly, 48-page kids' magazine which was distributed nationally by Xerox Education Publications and sold in schools.

Printed in the United States
by Baker & Taylor Publisher Services